WORLDVIEW GUIDE

MUCH ADO ABOUT NOTHING

Elizabeth Howard

canonpress
Moscow, Idaho

Published by Canon Press
P.O. Box 8729, Moscow, Idaho 83843
800.488.2034 | www.canonpress.com

Elizabeth Howard, *Worldview Guide for Much Ado About Nothing*
Copyright ©2018 by Elizabeth Howard.
Cited page numbers come from the Canon Classics edition of the play (2016),
www.canonpress.com/books/canon-classics.

Cover design by James Engerbretson
Cover illustration by Forrest Dickison
Interior design by Valerie Anne Bost and James Engerbretson

Printed in the United States of America.

A free end-of-book test and answer key are available for download at
www.canonpress.com/ClassicsQuizzes

Howard, Elizabeth, 1987- author.
Much ado about nothing worldview guide / Elizabeth Howard.
Moscow, Idaho : Canon Press, [2019].
LCCN 2019011339 | ISBN 9781947644335 (paperback : alk. paper)
LCSH: Shakespeare, William, 1564-1616. Much ado about nothing.
LCC PR2828 .H69 2019 | DDC 822.3/3--dc23
LC record available at https://lccn.loc.gov/2019011339

19 20 21 22 23 24 9 8 7 6 5 4 3

CONTENTS

INTRODUCTION

If a theatrical performance is primarily seen and heard, the main action in *Much Ado About Nothing* is principally overheard. The act of noting defines the play.[1] While this dependence on noting seems rather harmless if the task is tricking Beatrice and Benedick to fall in love, Claudio's mistaken noting threatens to upend the comedy and undo all of the matches. Can anything good come out of this chaos over "nothing"?

---

1. The verbal play between "noting" and "nothing" is not merely a spelling similarity; in Elizabethan English they were pronounced similarly. We might call them Elizabethan homophones. See Michael Best, "Masks; much ado about noting," *Internet Shakespeare Editions*, (Victoria, BC: University of Victoria, 2001-2010), http://internet-shakespeare.uvic.ca/m/lifetimes/plays/much%20ado%20about%20nothing/adomasks.html.

THE WORLD AROUND

While little is known about the personal details of Shake-speare's life, recent scholarship has given careful attention to the quality of education available to Shakespeare at the grammar school in Stratford-upon-Avon and the classical texts available to him in sixteenth-century England. Shakespeare would have known a number of classical mythologies, and Latin epics, lyrics, and narratives, like Ovid's *Metamorphoses*.[2] Shakespeare writes within an early modern tradition wherein the act of reading involved rewriting. Adaptation and imitation were the literary

---

2. For a survey of the range of classical texts in an early modern grammar school education, see Colin Burrow's excellent chapter, "Classical Influences," in *The Oxford Handbook of Shakespeare's Poetry* (Oxford University Press, 2013), 97-115. Also Thomas Baynes's "What Shakespeare Learnt at School," *Shakespeare studies, and essay on English dictionaries* (London: Longmans, Green, and co., 1894), *Shakespeare Online*, 20 Aug. 2000, http://www.shakespeare-online.com/biography/ whatdidshkread.html.

and pedagogical values of the day. There were as many
as seventeen variants of the slandered bride story when
Shakespeare wrote *Much Ado* at the end of the sixteenth
century.[3]

The themes of marriageability, potential sexual scandal,
and ambiguous exchanges with suitors had a particular
political relevance in Elizabethan England. One of the
pressing concerns of the day was Elizabeth I's status as the
unwed "Virgin Queen." In the latter half of Elizabeth's
reign, there certainly was "much ado" in England about
the possibility of a royal marriage that would restructure
England's international alliances and provide the Tudor
family with an heir to the throne. Three years after *Much
Ado* appeared as a quarto text, Elizabeth I died without a
husband or a biological heir.

Since the eighteenth-century, *Much Ado About Nothing*
has been dated to 1600, which was the date assigned to
the first quarto edition of the play.[4] It was likely written
just before then, since the names of the actors Kemp and
Cowley appear in the speech headings of Act 4, scene 2
instead of Dogberry and Verges, and Kemp had left the
acting troupe in 1599.[5]

---

3. William Shakespeare, *The New Oxford Shakespeare: Modern Critical
Edition: The Complete Works*, ed. Gary Taylor, John Jowett, Terri Bourus,
and Gabriel Egan, critical edition (Oxford: Oxford University Press,
2018), 1440.

4. William Shakespeare, *Much Ado About Nothing*, ed. David Stevenson
(New York: Signet, 1998), 150.

5. *The New Oxford Shakespeare*, 1440. For the names of Kemp and
Cowley in the quarto, see *Much Ado*, ed. David Stevenson, li. For
Kemp's departure from the company see William Shakespeare, *Much*

ABOUT THE AUTHOR

Baptismal records indicate that William Shakespeare was born in April of 1564. Shakespeare married Anne Hathaway, a woman eight years his senior, in 1582. After the birth of their first daughter Suzanna and their twins Hamnet and Judith, Shakespeare moved to London to continue his work as an actor and playwright. His relatively rapid rise to popularity aggravated his contemporaries, for Robert Greene appears to call him an "upstart crow" in his indirect address to Thomas Nashe, Christopher Peele, and Christopher Marlowe at the end of *Groatsworth of Wit* (1592).[6]

Ado about Nothing, ed. F. H. Mares, updated edition (Cambridge, UK: Cambridge University Press, 2003), 7.

6. That the "upstart crow" refers to Shakespeare is, however, contested by some scholars. See Daryl Piksen, "Was Robert Greene's 'Upstart Crow' the actor Edward Alleyn," *The Marlowe Society Research Journal* 6, 2009, https://www.marlowe-society.org/pubs/journal/downloads/rj06articles/jl06_03_pinksen_upstartcrowalleyn.pdf.

Within ten years, Shakespeare and his acting troupe, which included the well-known actor Richard Burbage, received their patronage from the Lord Chamberlain and took on the name the Lord Chamberlain's Men in 1594. They became the King's Men in 1603 when James I became their patron. Shakespeare helped to found the Globe Theater that same year, and he continued to enjoy a tenth share of the profits until his death on April 25, 1616. Shakespeare was buried in his hometown of Strafford-on-Avon, where his tombstone left an ominous warning:

> Good friend, for Jesus' sake forbear
> To dig the dust enclosed here.
> Blessed be the man that spares these stones
> And cursed be he that moves my bones.

His bones remain unmoved. After Shakespeare's death, two friends and actors in the King's Men, Henry Condell and John Heminges, edited and published Shakespeare's *First Folio* in 1623.

While Shakespeare, as Samuel Johnson noted, is primarily remembered for his drama, he also published three lengthy poems during his life: *Venus and Adonis* in 1593, *The Rape of Lucrece* in 1594, and *A Lover's Complaint* in 1609. His cache of 154 sonnets, written in the mid-nineties, was published in 1609.

WHAT OTHER NOTABLES SAID

Much Ado About Nothing is full of songs, which W.H. Auden praised for their "contributions to the dramatic structure" despite their "irrelevant" appearance, and therefore *Much Ado* has a strong presence in the long tradition of musical arrangements made for the songs of Shakespeare.[7] French composer Hector Berlioz turned the verbal sparring between Beatrice and Benedick into the opera *Béatrice et Bénédict* (1860-1862). Berlioz described his "two heroes Beatrice and Benedict [as] teasing and snapping at each other with elegance" in such a way as to "require extreme delicacy in performance."[8] In a 1898 review of *Much Ado* performed at St. James's Theatre, George

---

7. Quoted in *Much Ado*, ed. Stevenson, 125. For a nineteenth-century list of such songs, see William Shakespeare et al., *A List of All the Songs & Passages in Shakespere Which Have Been Set to Music*, Selections (London: Pub. for the New Shakspere society, by N. Trübner, 1884), https://catalog.hathitrust.org/Record/001454028.

8. *The New Oxford Shakespeare*, 1440.

Bernard Shaw expressed a similar concern, describing the play as "perhaps the most dangerous actor-manager trap in the whole Shakespearean repertory" since "its success depends on the way it is handled in performance."[9]

Lewis Carroll, however, complained that the largest liability in the play was the plot itself. According to Carroll, Claudio's slander at the wedding could have easily been refuted with "an alibi."[10] Despite that implausibility, *Much Ado About Nothing* was the personal favorite Shakespearean play of Charles Darwin's wife, Emma Darwin.[11]

The essayist William Hazlitt wryly commented on the political folly of his own day when he announced that "Dogberry and Verges, who are the inimitable specimens of quaint blundering and misprision of meaning" seem to have ascended "in the course of two hundred years… from the lowest to the highest offices in the state."[12]

9. *Much Ado*, ed. David Stevenson, 111.

10. *Much Ado*, ed. F. H. Mares, 169.

11. H. E. Litchfield, and Emma Darwin, *Wife of Charles Darwin: A Century of Family Letters* (Cambridge: The University Press, 2010), 3.

12. *The New Oxford Shakespeare*, 1440.

SETTING, CHARACTERS AND PLOT SUMMARY

- *Setting:* The story takes place within the city of Messina. The companions of Don Pedro have recently returned from the wars, and they have decided to rest at the home of Leonato, Prince of Messina.
- Leonato is the father of Hero and host to Don Pedro and his companions.
- Hero, the only child of Leonato, is soon engaged to Claudio, but the scheming of Don John threatens both her wedding day and any future prospect of marriage.
- Beatrice is Hero's loyal, feisty cousin who enjoys an ongoing "war of wit" with Don Pedro's companion, Signor Benedick.
- Don Pedro, also known as the Prince, is the head of the troop of soldiers who have arrived

at Leonato's house. He is a winsome leader, if overly trusting of his brother Don John.

- The impulsive Claudio has traveled with Don Pedro to Messina after the war, and has fallen in love with Leonato's daughter, Hero. His rash conclusions cause the principle drama in the play.
- Benedick is another companion to Don Pedro, and a self-proclaimed bachelor, who enjoys a lion's share of the lines and the majority of the verbal humor. He unwittingly falls in love with Beatrice and is, therefore, responsible for challenging Claudio after Claudio slanders Hero.
- The miserable Don John, half-brother to Don Pedro, funds any plots to harm the happy party in Messina. He further despises Claudio for the favor Don Pedro shows him.
- Conrad is the servant of Don John.
- Borachio, drunken friend of Conrad, is the author of the plot to slander Hero. He is also apprehended by the night watch while gloating with Conrad over his success.
- Dogberry is the constable in Messina. Although he is quick to confuse his audience through his endlessly jumbled homonyms, antonyms, and basic syntax, he desires to bring even the most insignificant forms of injustice to light.

- Verges is Dogberry's trusty assistant. He can be played as more or less competent than Dogberry.

With Don Pedro's victory over his brother's insurrection, a new sort of pursuit begins in the city of Messina: Claudio has his eye on Hero, the daughter of the host, Leonato. Meanwhile Hero's cousin, the feisty Beatrice, carries on her own verbal sparring with Benedick, and their friends conspire to trick them into falling in love to pass the time until Claudio and Hero's wedding day.

But not all is happy in Messina. Don John, bitter over his brother's victory and jealous of Don Pedro's favor toward Claudio, plots to ruin the wedding. With the help of Conrad, Don John hires Borachio to stage a scandal that will ruin Hero's reputation. The incompetent but ever vigilant constable Dogberry and his assistant Verges discover the author of mischief and slander, but they are too late to prevent a disastrously aborted wedding. Claudio, a rather rash and jealous young man, responds to Don John's "evidence" of Hero's infidelity just as Don John hoped he would: he shames Hero before the whole congregation at the wedding altar. Horrified, Hero collapses while Claudio, Don Pedro, and a (delighted) Don John storm off. The play threatens to end like the tragedy *Othello*, ruined by rumor and jealousy.

Friar Francis councils the miserable Hero, her speechless cousin Beatrice, and the outraged Leonato to publish the news that Hero has died from the shock of the slander to allow opportunity for truth to prevail and for Claudio to realize his grievous error. During the long, sad days of waiting, Beatrice gives up her jesting, receiving Benedick's comfort and help. Benedick, who has fallen in love with Beatrice, finds his attachment to her stronger than his friendship with Claudio and the Prince; at Beatrice's request he challenges Claudio to a duel.

Once the Constable and Dogberry are finally able to make their report understood and Don John is revealed to be a scoundrel, Claudio is quick to repent. Don Pedro insists that, as penance, Claudio marry a niece of his who, wonder of wonders, looks a lot like the "dead" Hero. Benedick drops his challenge. Claudio returns to the altar to find this "niece" is none other than Hero! With Claudio and Hero married, Benedick asks Beatrice to marry him as well—but not without a last bit of sparring from his soon-to-be bride.

WORLDVIEW ANALYSIS

Throughout *Much Ado*, Shakespeare examines the mechanism by which people "fall in love."[13] *Much Ado* often treats that "fall" rather literally. A trap involving eavesdropping or overhearing is set for an unsuspecting character; inevitably the character takes the "bait" by believing the truth of the rumor. This is how Hero and Ursula describe the way that they will persuade Beatrice to fall in love with Benedick: Hero explains that Cupid's "crafty" arrows wound "by hearsay" (3.1, p. 37), and when Ursula describes Beatrice as "a fish" coming to "devour the treacherous bait," Hero clarifies that it is "false-sweet bait that we lay for [her ear]" (3.1, p. 37).[14] At the end of their constructed conversation, designed for Beatrice to overhear,

13. In this way *Much Ado* shares an important theme with *Midsummer Night's Dream*, where Shakespeare imagines the chaos that ensues when magic potions dictate affections.

14. All citations to the play are given by act, scene, and page number of the Canon Press edition.

Ursula exults, "We have caught her, madam" (3.1, p. 40) to which Hero replies, "If it prove so, then loving goes by haps. / Some Cupid kills with arrows, some with traps" (3.1, p. 40). According to Ursula, to make someone fall in love, the god of love can either shoot someone with an "arrow of love," suggesting that they fall in love at "first sight," or rely on the power of hearsay or the praise of others. Don Pedro, who devised the scheme to "bring Signor Benedick and the Lady Beatrice into a mountain of affection" (2.1, p. 25), also claims the status of Cupid (2.1, p. 25). He argues that the party's capacity to trick Beatrice and Benedick into falling in love means that they have displaced Cupid himself and have become "the only love-gods" (2.1, p. 25), arranging and manipulating the affections of others.

Essentially all who participate in Don Pedro's plan make an important assumption about the mechanism of love: they all bear witness to the fact that falling in love is a highly mediated activity. In other words, standing between any two lovers, you can usually find some kind of mediator: another character, a book, a letter, perhaps rumors and hearsay, or, sometimes, diabolical plotting. "Cupid's arrows" and "Cupid's traps" are metaphorical and mythical descriptors for these mediators. In *Much Ado About Nothing*, one never simply falls in love.

"Making" someone fall in love, therefore, requires an act of invention or artistry, and if we attribute less noble motives, we might describe the action as artifice or fabrication. The slippery boundary between different kinds of "makers" (with the inspired muse on one side of the moral spectrum and sly liar on the other) is one of the most animated debates in Elizabethan criticism.[15]

Now, if less-than-truthful mediators can move characters to fall in love, the play suggests that the reverse outcome is also a possibility: one might fall *out* of love in the same way one fell in—by traps. Don John is delighted by Borachio's plan to call the maid-in-waiting, Margaret, to look out Hero's bedchamber window in an "unseasonable instant of the night" (2.3, p. 26). Borachio explains that Claudio will witness "proof enough" in the scene to believe that Hero is being sexually promiscuous with another man since Hero and Margaret look similar enough to be mistaken for each other. According to Borachio, "there shall appear such seeming truth of Hero's disloyalty that [Claudio's] jealousy shall be called assurance, and all the preparations overthrown" (2.3, p. 34-5). Borachio perfectly anticipates Claudio's reaction, as he later confides to Conrad: "Away went Claudio enraged, swore he would meet her [at the wedding], and there, before the whole congregation, shame her […] and send her home without a husband" (3.4, p. 27). Claudio disgraces Hero publicly because Don John tells him how to interpret a pantomime he witnessed of Hero's infidelity. As an evil mediator, Don John sabotages Hero and Claudio's relationship by masquerading as Claudio's friend. The play says as much

---

15. See Phillip Sidney's *A Defense of Poesy* (1595).

about choosing wise counselors as it comments on falling in love. Here, as in so many Shakespeare plays, "the companion of fools will suffer harm" because our companions inform the way we interpret what we see (Prov. 13:20).

When we hear that the experience of love is mediated in *Much Ado*, we might be tempted to describe Claudio's falling in love as an exception to this rule. His first words on stage are a declaration that he is in love with Hero, and he seems to have just met her. But notice that he declares his love *after* he has heard Don Pedro praise her beauty (1.1, p. 4). Claudio asks Benedick if he "noted" the daughter of Signor Leonato (1.1, p. 16); bachelor Benedick did not, but Don Pedro certainly did.[16] And he praises Hero again when Claudio asks his opinion (1.1, p. 7). Claudio even asks if Don Pedro is trying to "fetch [him] in" by praising Hero so highly (1.1, p. 7). Don Pedro's admiration of Hero might help explain why Claudio is quick to suspect that Don Pedro courts Hero for himself at Don John's suggestion (2.1, p. 19). Don John's report is, of course, false, since Don Pedro is a mediator helping Hero to fall in love with Claudio. The Prince has merely offered to "minister to love" (1.2, p. 10) by pretending to be Claudio so that he can convince Hero to marry Claudio.

While Don Pedro and Claudio's relationship demonstrates that love can be mediated in forms other than

---

16. Many thanks to my colleague, Joe Rigney, for first calling my attention to Claudio's affection for Hero which imitates the Prince's own interest in her.

deception, deceit is the play's favorite mediating structure for love. According to Graham Storey, "Deception
operates at every level of *Much Ado*; it is the common de-
nominator of the three plots, and its mechanisms—eavesdropping, mistakes of identity, disguises and maskings,
exploited hearsay—are the stuff of the play."[17]

To understand the implications of Storey's pronounce-
ment, it is helpful to compare *Much Ado* with some of its
sources and analogues. Among the seventeen wronged
bride narratives circulating when Shakespeare wrote
Much Ado, its most direct sources appear to be Joanot
Martorell's romance *Triant lo Blanch* (1490) and Matteo
Bandello's twenty-second story from his *Novelle* (1554).[18]
Alexander Pope cites Ariosto's *Orlando Furioso* as an early
source for *Much Ado*,[19] and John Harrington had translat-
ed *Orlando* into English verse in 1591, making it reason-
ably accessible to Shakespeare in English.[20] Others have
noted similarities between Claudio and Phedon from
Book II of *The Faerie Queene*.[21] In each of these source
narratives, deceit persuades a suitor to forsake his love, but
Shakespeare's *Much Ado* takes the sinister deceit of Don
John and pairs it with innumerable innocent traps and

17. Graham Storey, quoted. in *The New Oxford Shakespeare*, 1440.
18. Shakespeare, *Much Ado*, ed. Mares, 1. See also *The New Oxford
Shakespeare*, 1438–39.
19. Austin Warren, *Alexander Pope as Critic and Humanist* (Ann Arbor:
University of Michigan, 1963), 130.
20. *The New Oxford Shakespeare*, 1438–39.
21. Shakespeare, *Much Ado*, ed. Mares, 3.

plot-saving tricks—from flirtations at a masked dance and garden eavesdropping, to funeral rites conducted at the site of an empty grave.

The pairing of Don John's malevolent deceits with other "benevolent" deceits frames the play's "happy" ending. After Claudio publicly shames Hero and Hero faints, the Friar recommends that the house of Leonato pretend that she has died. When Hero's good name is cleared, Claudio seeks to do penance for his offense and Leonato asks that he hold a public vigil at her tomb and marry an unnamed cousin of Hero that is "almost a copy of my child that's dead" (5.1, p. 80). When Claudio sees her, he declares, "Another Hero!" (5.4, p. 89). At first this appearance of "another Hero" resolves the play's plot in a lighthearted direction. If we don't provide Claudio with a wife, the play is a tragedy. And from Claudio's perspective, the appearance of "another Hero" is a fortuitous happenstance; "another Hero" means that Claudio can perform the conditions to receive Leonato's forgiveness, and he will still end up with a wife as pretty as Hero and inherit Leonato's money. By disguising Hero as a double of herself, Leonato ensures that his daughter will be honorably married to her intended husband.

Nonetheless, this critical moment should cause the reader no little discomfort. "Another Hero," namely one speaking out Hero's chamber window, was the source of the original catastrophe in the play. Although different motives define the two "swapping Hero tricks," notice how similar the deceits are: Margaret seen as Hero and Hero seen as a-random-cousin-who-looks-just-like-Hero. (Incidentally, in the scene where Hero both speaks at length for herself and plays herself, she is busy tricking Beatrice.) Giving Claudio "another Hero" covers for the deceit of Hero's feigned death, but there is something profoundly unsatisfying in the continued deception. Deceits were funny, harmless tricks when Beatrice and Benedick fell in love. Once, however, Hero almost dies as a result of a trick, the play's entire disposition towards deceit shifts dramatically.

Since the play presents deceit as a powerful and potentially dangerous mediator in *Much Ado*, it raises questions about our human tendency to jump to conclusions. The plot relies upon characters who will "note" scraps of evidence placed in front of them, believe the evidence without further context, and extrapolate conclusions. The play is thus both the story of those who make much ado by noting and a story of those who make "much ado about nothing."

The theatre is a "place for seeing,"[22] but *Much Ado* plays with partial views and half sight. It is easy to overlook an important piece of information (like the fact that Hero isn't actually the woman in the window) when you are an interloper who is only "overhearing." The entire play functions as a commentary on the ways in which overhearing

---

22. Shakespeare, *Much Ado*, ed. Stephenson, 1.

is a failure of hearing. It is necessarily both hearing too much and, simultaneously, hearing too little.

The play then asks what power words might have in marring the truth. False words are a kind of "nothing" since they do not represent anything of substance. Nonetheless, they are powerful enough to kill, as Leonato charges Borachio: "With thy breath thou has killed mine innocent child" (5.1, p. 80). Leonato further expands those guilty of slander to include Count Claudio and Don Pedro: "I thank you, princes, for my daughter's death" (5.1, p. 80). As the play moves from seemingly harmless traps into malicious slanders, we ought to remember that none of the characters were even afraid of slander at the play's beginning. Beatrice, the character most incensed at Claudio's action, initially jokes that Benedick does nothing for the prince but devise "impossible slanders" (2.1, p. 18). By the end of the play, "impossible slanders" are no longer terms to be bandied about frivolously in the war of wit.

Much Ado offers a marked commentary on the frailty of love and the powers of mediators—those external, like Don John, and those internal, like the imagination of a jealous mind. But the play does not necessarily take a cynical position towards love. The position of the cynic is expressed by Claudio, who endeavors to eschew all mediation in love: "Therefore, all hearts in love use their own tongues; / Let every eye negotiate for itself / And trust no agent" (2.1, p. 19). Such a comment is not only cynical but also naive. Agents or mediators are a *part* of the fabric of love. Human relationships cannot help relying on them. Rather than despising love because it is often mediated by the influence of another, the play puts a cast of mediators on display, warning, albeit with a lighter touch than on the stage of a tragedy, that counselors with evil motives can exert a great deal of persuasion on those who are not discerning and patient. The play calls for us to discipline our own imaginations and to use them to care better for others than for ourselves.

If Claudio and Hero's hasty marriage threatens to make us cynics on matters of the heart, we must remember their foil: the happy union of Benedick and Beatrice. While Claudio falls in and out of and back in love again, Shakespeare offers a deeply satisfying love story of fierce verbal wars converted to faithful loves. Shakespeare uses the full duration of play to work out that transformation, rewarding the patience of his audience who waits so long (and the other characters who work so hard) to see these two publicly confess their love for one another.

The romantic satisfaction is particularly pronounced in Beatrice, who has been hurt in love by Benedick before (1.1, p. 5; 2.1, p. 22) and, like Benedick, begins the play an avowed skeptic towards love. By Act 4.1, Beatrice's willingness to trust Benedick with her pain betrays a growing confidence in the capacities of love. Beatrice has come to believe that a true love will defend her and her suit, and her appeal to Benedick matures him from comic love-sick suitor to a brave advocate.

Shakespeare's comedy offers further surprising satisfaction in the bumbling Dogberry. Of course Dogberry's mistakes are the source of as much verbal entertainment as the witty repartee of Benedick and Beatrice (cf. "Thou wilt be condemned into everlasting redemption for this," 4.2, p. 69), but Shakespeare also uses the "fool" to discover the villainy of Don John and bring about justice. Precisely because Dogberry's men only *accidentally* overhear Borachio's conversation with Conrad, the interrogation scene demonstrates that truth will make itself known in the end despite the worst incompetence. Here as in many other places in Shakespeare, "Truth will out" (*Merchant of Venice* 2.2.64).

QUOTABLES

1. "O Lord, he [Benedick] will hang upon him like a disease: he is sooner caught than the pestilence, and the taker runs presently mad. God help the noble Claudio! If he have caught the Benedick, it will cost him a thousand pound ere a' be cured."

    ~Beatrice, 1.1, p. 3

2. "I had rather be a canker in a hedge than a rose in his grace, [...]. I am trusted with a muzzle and enfranchised with a clog; therefore I have decreed not to sing in my cage. If I had my mouth, I would bite; if I had my liberty, I would do my liking: in the meantime let me be that I am and seek not to alter me."

    ~Don John, 1.3, p. 12

3. "Friendship is constant in all things, save in the office and affairs of love."

    ~Claudio, 2.1, p. 19

4. "I may chance have some odd quirks and remnants of
    wit broken on me, because I have railed so long against
    marriage: but doth not the appetite alter? A man loves
    the meat in his youth that he cannot endure in his age.
    Shall quips and sentences and these paper bullets of
    the brain awe a man from the career of his humour?
    No, the world must be peopled. When I said I would
    die a bachelor, I did not think I should live till I were
    married. Here comes Beatrice. By this day! she's a fair
    lady: I do spy some marks of love in her."

    ~Benedick, 2.3, p. 34

5. "If it proves so, then loving goes by haps:
    Some Cupid kills with arrows, some with traps."

    ~ Hero, 3.1, p. 40

6. "Kill Claudio."

    ~ Beatrice, 4.1, p. 66

7. "O villain! thou wilt be condemned into everlasting
    redemption for this."

    ~ Dogberry, 4.2, p. 69

21 SIGNIFICANT QUESTIONS AND ANSWERS

1. How might the initial reference to the end of "the wars" be an important piece of information for establishing the setting of the play? (1.1.6)

> This play is a comedy. War and political conflict do little to interrupt the plot or trouble the characters. Instead, it is the wars that have happily brought Don Pedro's men to the house of Signor Leonato. War is the foil to the frivolities of this play: the masked ball, the songs of Balthasar, and the efforts to trick Beatrice and Benedick. Furthermore these "wars" serve an initial counterpoint to the "merry war" (1.1, p. 3) between Beatrice and Benedick with its endless "skirmishes of wit" (1.1, p. 3). Benedick may boast of his enduring interest in being a bachelor soldier, but he cannot help but bandy words with Beatrice.

2. How might we characterize the cadre that Don Pedro
    has brought with him? Are there any characters that
    give us reason to pause?

> Claudio's speedy infatuation with Hero and his
> instant dismay at his inability to pursue her call
> attention to the hasty judgment that defines his
> personality. Benedick's absolute disinterest in
> the beautiful Hero and his whole-hearted verbal
> sparring with Beatrice demonstrate his committed
> bachelorhood early in the play. Don Pedro's nobility
> is apparent in his formal interactions with Leonato.
> By the end of Act 1, we know that Don John, who
> describes himself as a "plain-dealing villain" (1.3, p.
> 12), will be trouble for the party in Messina.

3. Why is Don John so dour?

> There are at least two elements to note in his speech
> on 1.3, p. 12. First, Don John boasts that it is his
> nature to be morose and moody: "Let me be that
> I am" (1.3, p. 12). This melancholy or "ill-natured
> temperament" was understood in the pre-modern
> world to result from an imbalance in the humors
> in the body.[23] But his attitude is also affected by
> his situation. There seems to have been a quarrel
> between himself and his brother (perhaps related to

---

23. See the early modern publications of Hippocrates's *De Humoribus*,
(1525) or Galen's *De temperamentis libri tres* (1545) and Shakespeare's
contemporary, Thomas Elyot and his treatise, *Castel of Helth* (1541), or
The World of Shakespeare's Humors, U.S. National Library of Medicine,
https://www.nlm.nih.gov/exhibition/shakespeare/fourhumors.html.

Don John's role in the "wars" given his reaction to
Claudio ("That young start-up hath all the glory of
my overthrow," 1.3, p. 13), and Don John now considers himself a prisoner under his brother's control:
"I have decreed not to sing in my cage" (1.3, p. 12).
Don John is also Pedro's illegitimate brother (5.1, p.
77), so presumably he has been passed over as the
named heir. He is also jealous of Claudio's favor in
Don Pedro's eyes (1.3, p. 13). We might contrast
Don John's unwillingness to change his disposition
with Benedick's advice to Beatrice: "Serve God, love
me, and mend" (5.3, p. 85).

4. In Beatrice and Benedick's war of wit, their words, including their names, are loaded with double meanings.
What irony might we notice in the name Beatrice?

Beatrice, the Italian variant of the Latin name
Beatrix, literally means "bringer of happiness."
When explaining why she speaks "all mirth and
no matter," she explains that she was born under
a dancing star in a merry hour (2.1, p. 24). At the
same time, there is a tension in Beatrice's mirth because her so-called "happy" jesting is often barbed
and bewildering. Benedick is the primary target of
Beatrice's verbal wit, and he certainly suffers shame
under her relentless attacks (2.1, p. 22), but Don
Pedro suffers too (2.1, p. 24), and Leonato and
Antonio fear she will never find a husband due to
her sharp tongue (2.1, p. 15). If no one is safe from
your verbal attacks, even if you meant it all in fun, is
it really fair to call you "the bringer of happiness"?

5. What about the name Benedick?

> Benedick's name is made from two Latin words,
> bene and dictus, and means "well-spoken" or
> "good words." If by "well-spoken" we mean that
> Benedick is clever with his words, he proves to be
> so. Benedick enters the stage in Act 1 needling
> Leonato before he encounters Beatrice (1.1, p. 4)
> and teases Claudio for falling for Hero (1.1, p. 6).
> Such words might qualify as "well-spoken" in the
> sense of "Ouch! That was a good one!" Furthermore,
> he alone can find a fitting retort for Beatrice, and
> his retorts include calling Beatrice "Lady Disdain"
> (1.1, p. 4)—a description of her that other charac-
> ters borrow (cf 3.1, p. 38), a "rare parro- teacher"
> (1.1, p. 5) with claws (1.1, p. 5), and a "harpy" (2.1,
> p. 22). But because his words are harsh, there is
> a profound sense in which they are hardly "good
> words" like the fitting words described in Proverbs
> as "apples of gold in settings of silver" (Prov. 25:11).

> In the end Benedick lives up to his name better
> than at first. He comforts Beatrice in her grief (4.1,
> p. 65). His challenge to Claudio causes him to own
> the wrong he has done to Hero (see 5.1, p. 76).

6. What is a major running pun in Beatrice and
    Benedick's verbal war?

> One of the most common tropes that Beatrice and
> Benedick use is the metaphor of illness. Beatrice
> describes Benedick as a "disease" worse than an

everlasting plague (1.1, p. 3), and she fears that Claudio will catch "the Benedick" if he spends too much time with him (1.1, p. 3). At the play's end both invoke the other's love sickness (5.4, p. 90), and Beatrice boasts that she will marry Benedick if only to save his life because he was dying of "a consumption" (5.4, p. 90). Others enjoy punning off his name; Margaret suggests "Carduus Benedictus" might cure Beatrice's cold, borrowing the medicinal and curative connotations of the name, knowing that Beatrice suffers primarily from the passion of love (3.5, p. 52).

7. When did this "merry war" between Beatrice and Benedick start?

The play doesn't answer this question directly, but Beatrice alludes to an answer. Don Pedro jokes that she has "lost the heart of Signor Benedick" when Benedick complains that he would do literally anything rather than talk to Beatrice, but Beatrice's answer to him is surprisingly serious: "Indeed, my lord, he lent it me awhile, and I gave him use for it, a double heart for his single one. Marry, once before he won it of me with false dice; therefore your Grace may well say I have lost it" (2.1, p. 22). Beatrice suggests here that Benedick either betrayed her confidence or made her doubt his love some time ago (1.1, p. 5). Her ruthless jabs seem to originate in her hurt feelings and injured pride.

8. Who wins the verbal war between Beatrice and Benedick?

> We could determine the victor by tallying who wins each of the individual skirmishes. For example, Beatrice concedes to Benedick in their first fight: "You always end with a jade's trick. I know you of old" (1.1, p. 5). Beatrice certainly wins the second verbal fight at the masked ball when Benedick is in disguise, since he cannot speak in his own defense, nor can he give himself away (2.1, p. 18, 20). Another way to determine victor is to identify the first to fall in love (Benedick) or the first to capitulate to the serious request of the other (Benedick agrees to duel his close friend Claudio at Beatrice's behest). At the play's end, Benedick calls the truce on their war by "stopping" Beatrice's mouth with a kiss—an echo of Beatrice's advice to Hero when Claudio first proposed (5.4, p. 91, cf. 2.1, p. 23).

9. Why is a masked ball a particularly fitting setting for the first wooing scene?

> It is key to remember that this play is about noting and deceit. During the masked ball, the characters pretend to deceive and mistake each other). In the flurry of disguises on stage, Claudio first believes Don John's deceit that Don Pedro is selfishly wooing for himself. The problem in Messina is not the masks at the party; the masks just call attention to time-worn adage that "appearances can be deceiving."

10. What motivates Don Pedro and the others to trick Benedick and Beatrice into falling in love?

> They want to see their friends happily married, and Leonato's guests are looking for a way to divert themselves until Claudio and Hero's wedding. Mischief-making is never far from a group of friends with time on their hands.

11. What is particularly ironic about the success of Borachio and Don John's plan to convince Claudio of Hero's "unfaithfulness"?

> Claudio should know better than to trust Don John; Don John has already deceived Claudio once over Don Pedro's wooing at the masked ball. "Fool me once, shame on you. Fool me twice, shame on me," so the saying goes.

12. Why would Claudio publicly defame the woman he loved so much?

> The scene at the wedding raises significant questions about Claudio's character and the quality of his love for Hero. We might interpret his actions as a result of his haste: he fell in love in an instant and can, it seems, fall of out of love just as quickly. We might also consider his jealous nature. Jealousy is quick to suspect others. Love, by contrast, "always believes, always hopes" (1 Cor. 13:7). In either case, Claudio thinks of himself and his own reputation before others. Were he principally considering

Hero's well-being, he would have acted more like Joseph, who was "of a mind to put [Mary] away quietly" when he discovered that she was pregnant with someone else's child (Matt. 1:19).

13. What would a charge of infidelity mean for Hero?

Historically the social costs for infidelity were much higher for a woman than a man. By publicly declaring that Hero had been false to him with another man, he ruined any chance of a respectable marriage for her, and, without the success of the friar's plan and her father's additional intervention, she would have needed to live a secluded life (Cf. 4.1, p. 64).

14. Identify the shrewd aspects of the Friar's plan. Is there anything disconcerting about it?

The Friar is a keen observer of human nature, and he has a remarkable grasp of imagination's influence on memory—what he calls the "study of imagination" (4.1, p. 64), but his entire plan depends upon Claudio and the city of Messina transferring their sense of guilt over "killing" an innocent maid into veneration for her. We call this victimizing followed by venerating "scapegoating," and we see it primarily in pagan mythologies where the victim blamed for causing some plague or disaster is later venerated as a goddess. Scapegoating is a social mechanism that bypasses the need for repentance and forgiveness, which makes it strange for the Friar to recommend it.

15. Everyone wants to duel Claudio. How do the repeated challenges expand the play's definition of manhood?

> Notice who is most enraged by his actions: Beatrice and old Antonio—the characters least able to defend Hero's honor by challenging Claudio to a duel. After Claudio slanders Hero, Beatrice, in agony for her cousin, declares, "O God, that I were a man" (4.1, p. 67) because she wishes she could challenge Claudio. She also rebukes Benedick for swearing his love to her by his hand instead of using that hand to punish Claudio. Her desperation and Antonio's demeaning names for Claudio and Don Pedro as "boyes (sic), apes, braggarts, jacks, milksops […] scrambling, out-facing, fashion-monging boys" (5.1, p. 74) emphasize Claudio's immaturity in his actions at the wedding. Benedick also calls Claudio a "boy" for his interest in "gossip-like humor" rather than justice (5.1, p. 77). The contrast between Claudio's stupid mockery, "God bless me from a challenge," and Benedick's serious charge, "I will make it good how your dare, with what you dare, and when you dare," could not be more stark (5.1, p. 76). In *Much Ado*, swords do not necessarily make soldiers.

16. Is Claudio guilty as charged for slandering Hero's good name?

> A good name is more valuable "than riches" (Prov. 22:1), thus slander, or a false public declaration about someone else's character, is a serious offense against one's neighbor. Because Claudio reported

what he believed to be true, he did not *intend* to
accuse Hero falsely like Don John did. Nonetheless,
Claudio made a public report before verifying
what he had seen. His information was false, so he
spreads a serious falsehood about Hero's character.

17. Is Leonato a good father to Hero?

Consider Leonato's introduction of Hero when
Don Pedro asks if she is his child: "Her mother
hath many times told me so" (1.1, p. 4). His comment casts unnecessary suspicion on the faithful-
ness of Hero's mother. Similarly the vehemence
in his tirade against Hero at the wedding suggests
that he has little faith in her (4.1, p. 61-2). Finally
Leonato considers himself the primary sufferer at
the wedding (much like Claudio had), and Antonio
even rebukes him for it (5.1, p. 72). We might
contrast his reaction with the Friar's belief in her
testimony and his care for Hero in her suffering.

18. How do Dogberry and Verges catch the real villainy when nobles fail to do so?

Dogberry cannot communicate clearly, but the fact
that even he is able to uncover the crime of Don
John suggests the folly of the nobility of Messina.
If Dogberry can catch the criminals, *how much more*
ought Don Pedro, Claudio, and the rest of the party
to have identified the plot of Don John.

19. When does Claudio repent for his actions? Explain.

Some point to Benedick's challenge as the moment
when Claudio recognizes the wrong he has done.
It certainly does not occur before that point, since
Claudio and Don Pedro both mock the outrage
of Leonato and Antonio when Benedick arrives
(5.1, p. 75). Others point to the tears he sheds at
Hero's tomb. Others are more skeptical yet; they
argue Claudio never actually repents because he too
willingly accepts a proxy wife, "Another Hero!" (5.4,
p. 89).

20. Does Claudio deserve to marry Hero in the end?

Some consider the marriage the act of reconcilia-
tion and forgiveness between Claudio and Hero;
they are quick to defend Hero's enduring love for
Claudio. Many, however, find this play's ending
completely unsatisfactory since Hero willingly
marries the man who defamed her. As a nineteenth-century German dramaturge objected,
"Here is no stuff of a comedy. A girl slandered and
ill-treated to an unutterable extent is not an object
to awaken merriment. And it is degrading that she
should finally, without hesitation, marry her slan-
derer."[24] The fact that Claudio "repents" of his error
to some degree before it is "too late" (i.e., Hero was
just hiding; she wasn't actually dead) keeps *Much
Ado* from becoming a tragedy. Had she died, this

24. Shakespeare, *The New Oxford Shakespeare*, 1437.

play would have been a tragedy. Shakespeare wrote that tragedy—it is called *Othello*.[25]

21. What are some of Beatrice and Benedick's other tropes?

Poets often ask what the "food" of love might be. Beatrice and Benedick consider verbal sparing as a form of sustenance. Beatrice suggests that the jokes she levels at his expense are like "food" to feed her "disdain" (1.1, p. 4). Beatrice, meanwhile, teases Benedick for his weak stomach. She explains that when he is teased he becomes so sad he cannot eat (2.1, p. 18). Benedick meanwhile complains to Don Pedro that he cannot endure the "dish" "Lady Tongue" (2.1, p. 22). Here Benedick refers both to the source of Beatrice's insults (her words proceed from her tongue) and the intention of her insults. He imagines her insults as a plate of tongue prepared just for him. He cannot eat what he is served.

---

25. The two plays are particularly powerful when performed or read in close proximity. The Oxford Shakespeare Festival 2018, for example, paired the two plays in a back-to-back performance to highlight their similarities.

FURTHER DISCUSSION AND REVIEW

Master what you have read by reviewing and integrating the different elements of this classic.

SETTING AND CHARACTERS
Be able to compare and contrast the personalities (including strengths, weaknesses, and mannerisms) of each character. Which characters change over the course of the play? Which do not?

PLOT
Be able to describe the beginning, middle, and end of the play along with specific details that move the plot forward and make it compelling.

CONFLICT
Go through the character list and describe the tension between any and all main characters. Then, think about

whether any characters have internal conflict (in their own minds). Is there any overt conflict (fighting), or conflict with impersonal forces?

THEME STATEMENTS

Be able to describe what this classic is telling us about the world. Is the message true? What truth can we take from the plot, characters, conflict, and themes (even if the author didn't believe that truth)? Do any objects take on added meaning because of repetition or their place in the story (i.e., do any objects become symbols)? How does the author use perspective, tone, and irony to tell the truth?

Compose your own theme statement about some element, large or small, of this classic. Then, use the Bible and common sense to address the truth of that theme statement. Identify your own key words or borrow from the following list as your starting point: *The mechanism of love; Appearances, eavesdropping, and noting; Friendship and loyalty and its limits; Deceit and trickery; Jealousy; Baseless judgment; Recompense; Repentance and penitence.*

TAKING THE CLASSICS QUIZ

Once you have finished the worldview guide, you can prepare for the end-of-book test. Each test will consist of a short-answer section on the book itself and the author, a short-answer section on plot and the narrative, and a long-answer essay section on worldview, conflict, and themes.

Each quiz, along with other helps, can be downloaded for free at www.canonpress.com/ClassicsQuizzes. If you have any questions about the quiz or its answers or the Worldview Guides in general, you can contact Canon Press at service@canonpress.com or 208.892.8074.

ABOUT THE AUTHOR

Elizabeth Howard is an adjunct faculty member at Bethlehem College & Seminary and is pursuing her PhD in English at the University of Minnesota. She has taught a range of literature, rhetoric, composition, and language courses at The Potter's School and Mars Hill Academy. She and her husband Zach, who also teaches at Bethlehem, have two daughters.

www.ingramcontent.com/pod-product-compliance
Lightning Source LLC
Chambersburg PA
CBHW071936020426
42331CB00010B/2900